Celebrate Connections!

Marcia

THE
COLOR CONNECTION

Written by Marcia Harris & Lisa Gray

Illustrations by Lindsey Burwell

dedicated to ART teachers everywhere

Once upon a time, in the land of Black and White, there lived a friendly creature named Mr. Purple.

Mr. Purple was cool and confident and he loved the town of
Black and White.
If everyone could learn to work and play together, it would
be perfect.

The problem was that ever since he could remember
(and that was a very long time),
the town of Black and White had been divided in half.

On one side - the East Side - lived the fiery Mr. Red, the cool Mr. Blue, and the always cheerful Ms. Yellow.

They thought they were very superior because they were the
PRIMARY colors and PRIMARY means FIRST.
They believed they should always be FIRST in line,
FIRST with the newest fashions, FIRST to try new foods,
FIRST in everything.

They even chose to live on the East side of town because the
sun rises in the East and they'd be the
FIRST to greet each new day.

On the West side of town lived Mr. Purple and his friends,
neat and clean Mr. Green and outspoken Mrs. Orange
--- the SECONDARY colors.

They were happy living on the West side of town
- every night they enjoyed a beautiful sunset.
Yet they also knew that everything they did was only second best
according to the PRIMARIES.

This was the problem Mr. Purple puzzled over.
Wouldn't it be more fun if they could all
live, work, and play together?
Could one little purple creature, a secondary color at
that --- make a difference?

Mr. Purple thought and thought.
What could bring everyone together?
What if he had a party?

But why would the PRIMARIES come to a party he planned?
They'd only think it was second rate and not worth their time.
Maybe --- if there was free food,
good music and dancing, games and prizes
--- he decided to give it a try.

To his surprise everyone said YES!!

The day of the party was bright and sunny and the park was all decorated and looked very festive. But, as the guests arrived, they all stayed in their own little groups.

Mr. Purple wasn't happy.
His plan to bring everyone together wasn't working.
And to top it off, it started to rain.

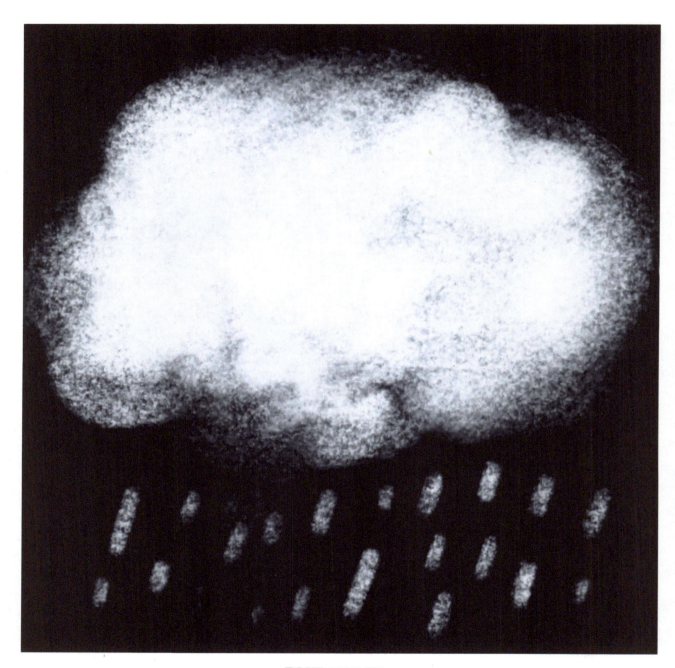

BUT WAIT...

Where Mr. Blue was touching Ms. Yellow, they became
--- GREEN

Where Mr. Red was touching Ms. Yellow, they became
--- ORANGE.

Where Mr. Blue was touching Mr. Red they became
--- PURPLE

Mr. Purple was the first to notice and he yelled,
"Look Friends!
There's a little bit of you in each of us.
We're all related!"

The PRIMARIES saw that this was true and they started to laugh.
"Weren't we silly not to get along?
If we work and play together,
the land of Black and White will be a BEAUTIFUL place!"

And it was ...

CPSIA information can be obtained
at www.ICGtesting.com
Printed in the USA
JSHW072358120423
39908JS00004BA/10